REVOLUTIONARY THOUGHTS

From The Mind of a Radical

Updated Version

Brother Ali-Hotep

© 2010 Brother Ali-Hotep All rights reserved.

No part of this book may be reproduced, stored in a retrieval system, or transmitted by any means without the written permission of the author.

A POETS' PLEDGE

There is an important saying that goes:

"Words mean more than what is set on paper
It takes the human voice to infuse them with shades of deeper meaning"

Well, that is the sole duty of a poet
Whose skillful wit and verbal mastery of normal stanzas,
Limericks,
Line numbers
And metaphors
Made to catch the attention
And entice the curiosity
Of true lovers of poetry
All over the world
We attract the deepest of closed minds
The strongest of curious souls
The laziest of unawakened consciences
And the highest of high spirits
With our literary genius and demeanor
We always give our one hundred and ten percent
Of our poetic blood, sweat and tears
To reach, teach and inspire
Open closed eyes and improvise the normal common sense
With truth and honesty
Instantly causing widespread thresholds in the mental state
Of the poetry haters
Who are still stuck with the same unclear notion
That real poets will never get paid
Nor receive the recognition that other performers have
But as I speak for my poetic brothers and sisters all over the world
I say the hell with all you poetry bashers
Look at you
You can't even write a simple stanza, limerick or a sentence that rhyme
You still do not understand that
True poetry is a cure for today's continued miseries
If lifts the unmovable spirits
Warms the coldest of hearts
And miraculously heals the deepest of emotional bruises
For we as real and dedicated poets,
We will be
The watchtowers of the alley,
The truth spitters from the projects,
The unclosed eyes of the neighborhood
The ever-beating heart of the street corner
And

The powerful voice of the ghetto
As long as there are great spoken word artists with the voices so loud and proud
Lyrical minds so razor sharp and focused
And
A deep and everlasting love for giving audiences what they want to experience
We, the poetic masters from around the world will continue to inform, educate, inspire and entertain
For that, we have the ultimate edge
And that is a true poets' pledge.

© 2009 Corey Ali Copeland

AMERICA SHEDS ITS TEARS

I see America shedding it tears
Crying…
Because of the damned fears that constantly plague is precious shores
For over a hundred years
Like the foul and unpleasant stench of slavery raised its ugly head

Spreading chaos throughout the moral fabric of conscience in my brothers and sisters
Causing them incursive pain and irritating crate like blisters
To the weakened soles of their feet and ankles
Bounded in shackles made of the most hardened steel
Set upon by those who want to use us like motherfucking cattle
Dominating our free will to survive and fight and continually degrading our self-esteem like we ain't shit to them in the first place
Kinda like a lying ass Republican senator giving the public a deaf ear
While sucking the dick of his leader, the forgetful Dubya to be morally cleansed
For my people, it don't make no damn sense
For I see America shedding its tears
Crying endlessly….
Because the blood of its children flowing out of control without warning
Like a polluted river of toxic waste wasting lives and taking pure and sweet memories of the childhood dreams that many children thought they can get them out of the ghetto
That eerie dark wasteland of endless street corners and rat-infested allies
You got every drug pusher and every pimp on every sideway
Every prostitute haunting every decent hard working brother for the feel of cash hard cash
Every Jackson, every Grant, every fucking Franklin
Then you got every dope fiend and basehead
Crackhead and heroin addict
Scheming for the stash of weed, meth and angel dust
Causing big dreams made by those who want to make a change
To just go up in smoke
And then they get high
So high
Until they are D.O.A. and fade away
Like sand on the beach
For I say I see America shedding its tears
Still crying and weeping
Weeping endlessly because the threat of Armageddon is coming and it's coming near like hordes of demons wreaking havoc over unsuspecting regions
Drowning its streets with raw and dirty waters that choke up the vast fabric of Black awareness like deep puddles of mud
Plaguing our precious communities with plain old bullshit and filth on their billboards
Got my brothers and sisters thinking rapidly and start to realize that we ain't taking any sub-cultural shit anymore!
Time for them to wash and cleanse our mindsets and start anew with a fresh dialogue

For I still see America shedding its tears
Crying like a motherless child….
As a brother in a fucked up society
I see America's tears with my own eyes
Because the demented powers that be who ruled her over eight years ago constantly making life even more difficult then it was in the 60's when many of our people gave their lives in order for the next generation to survive and prosper
Before Obama's light shine on the White House,
We were victims of a constantly misguided government which are full of liars and false prophets galore
Every politician kissing Bush's ass with a dick
While my people are the only ones getting screwed
And dying in their wars
Worst of all, we've had being "corcered" to their way of operation
While still searching for our means of salvation
So tell me
Why we are so obsessed with reality shows, the bling bling and using the B and N words to be totally hip to what's going on without getting back to basics
Like a village working collectively to raise a child
So that the seed can be a mature and better person
My brothers and sisters, hear me!
Let us be free of the ever continuing nonsense and begin a new sense of pride
To educate, inspire and uplift a whole new generation of youth
So they don't had to be jailed, falsely accused, being tricked into a state of misjudgment and being pawns in a establishment jam
Let them be the light of our hope and the beacon of our neighborhood
And then, finally…..
We can see America stop shedding its tears
So could someone get her some tissue, please?!!!!

© 2009 Corey Ali Copeland

CAN YOU FEEL IT?

Can you feel it?
Can you feel it, brothers and sisters?
Can you feel the winds of change passing along?
Can you feel the echoes of freedom ringing in your ears?
The buried souls of my ancestors calling me ten to a thousand fold to come
Into the light of hope
Can you feel the cries of the tribes flowing from the burial ground to
The polluted city air the smothered scattered emotions and unaccomplished
dreams
Can you feel the chants of the warriors hovering through the crowds
To hear them whispering
The words of solidarity
Action
And unity
For all
Can your feel the voices of my people heard through the ghettos of the city
To the villages of the motherland
Screaming
"We want to be free!"
"We want to be free!'
"Free!"
Can you feel the drums of the circles beating hard?
So that the corpses of deceased revolutionaries rise up
Rise Up!
Rise Up!
So they can walked and roamed through the damned streets from which
their legacies have been expired
Due to the wicked forces' collaboration to fuck up this planet and
to corrupt everything peaceful and just on it
Can you feel the tears of Mother Africa as they rolling down like a stream of blood
flowing from the heads of our griots
Eradicated by the evil grip of colonialism, apartheid and massacre that plagued us
for more than 400 years
Yet, we are still feeling its ever continuing effect
Can you feel the sobering cries of our youth howling through insensitive ears of
those who want to turn back to flow of revolutionary change?
Can you feel the coming of one million Black men with unified fists of liberation?
Can you feel the chill of power hissing in the dark storm hovering the horizon
with the call of sweet bonding?

Can you feel the spirits of King Tut, Chaka Zulu, Douglass, Sojourner Truth,
Tubman, Wells, Marcus, Martin, Malcolm, Kwame, HJ. Rap Brown and other
scholars of revolutionary dialouge
Screaming through the corridors of history
Blinded by the opinions of so-called historians
Who only believe in "His-story"
While our moral state of mind are subjected by "areas of interest"
Which are totally full of nonsense and of course
Bullshit
What I am saying is
Can you feel the tides of solution changing?
Can you feel the tortured lives of Black men, women and children
surge with their cries of retaliation and pain?
Can you feel the essence of the great tribes chanting their hymns of survival?
Can you hear one million warriors screaming for retribution against a currant
corrupt regime
Whose one and only purpose to systematically persecute and eliminate every free
thinking radical
Who don't subject to their kind of rule
Tell me
Can you feel the wave of hope passing through us?
Can you feel the sea of positivity with a powerful tidal wave destroying every
stench of negativity?
Can you feel the light of wisdom shining on a world of hearsay?
But furthermore,
Can you feel the power of our people?
The voice of a new generation of poets and poetesses
The truth…
The heart of a radical…
The love for yourself…
Brothers and sisters
The time for revolution is coming
And it is near
Question is…
Can you feel it?
Can you feel it?
Can you?

© 2006 Corey Ali Copeland

DE-PROGRAMMING OF A NIGGATRON

Too many niggatrons running rampant and out of control
Since the ending the horrible slave mentality
Which is secretly sucked into us by the ever-going clouds of Anglo-Saxon culture
They constantly hide in many places
Conceal themselves with many faces and dare to never leave any traces
Only to wait for the right moment to let loose on an unexpected world and be programmed by their corrupted white-collared "Slave Magnates"
To seek out and entice
Or shall I say brainwash
Any righteous brother or sister into their sick ass web of deception, agony and anarchy
Confusing their conscience into sadly thinking that this world is a better place
While we, the strong minded, know that this is an ever-turning ball of confusion
Still turning with wars and conflicts continuing to put a dent on modern day civilization
Niggatrons are still programmed by racist mindset computer chips which are activated when real brothers question their "blackness"
Instead, they pack some heat and shoot up blocks and cause a shit load of bloodshed
Leaving a generation of innocent lives dead
Dealing crack, weed and other dirty drugs on the corner in the dead of night
Some of them want to be gangsters, crooks, hustlers and thugs
Having so many children with no ounce of care
Fucking up the core of child welfare
Fools becoming super pimps with big dicks and dirty women becoming hoes with nasty tricks
Seducing conscious brothers with that nasty infected sweet spot that makes wanna holler
But still, niggatrons are still blinded like Old Man Ruckus on the Boondocks
Always worship the sick agenda in which they put upon us to hold us down and have us harassed by their blue-colored foot soldiers
Only for them to reduce our lifespan by a third or maybe a half
Causing a massive bloodbath of a people by a race who don't give a fuck about us
So tell me....
How can we constantly re-program the mind of a sellout?
Well, it's just that simple
First, we kidnap a niggatron from his daily routine of causing mass damage to the people
Then, secluding him from reality into a dark corner of the mind where no one can find him

We begin the first phase of re-programming by stripping away the niggatron of his manhood
Plaguing him to succumb to his insecurity just like a child with no mother or father to watch him grow
Strapping him down to a chair with the shackles of slavery
The same ones that the bastard slave mongers use to hold us down in their stinking plantations
Make that fool submit to images of the horrors and suffering the oppressors place among us
Causing him to panic, shiver and sweat
Also forcing him to develop major mental paranormal relapse
Shaken and comatose to the fact that it is his own self-hate and loyalty for his master that got him messed up in the first place
Kissing his ass
Sucking his big white dick
Being his personal bitch or hoe
Assisting him in making life so damn miserable for the rest of us
Can't have a damn say in our way
Can't marry own our women
We can't even fight or protest for our own rights
Because of his sellout ass
His de-programming session is ongoing
So that fool can't escape the fact that he's turning his back on his own
Just for the love of his savior
The plantation king
The corruptor
The damn swindler
His brain, which is psychologically damaged by a bigot white dialogue
Will be separated from the cerebellum
Only to be morally and pathologically washed from the Old World bullshit that was fed to us by those stuck-up sellout educators
His body will be branded and scarred like a piece of meat left to be molded by the worst bacteria
Eyes looking stoned and blurred
Only to see a collage of great Black history waiting to be transmitted into his psyche
Still trying to be resistant to the fact that he is a King among Kings instead of a slave
The niggatron will do anything to remain loyal to his damn oppressors by lying, scheming and denying his own self, history or culture
But that won't stop the re-education process of the de-programming session
Which to systematically eradicate the white devil dialogue out of his mindset and then cleanse the cerebrum of all things wicked and un-pure

Until he realize…
He is a longer a controlled modern slave corrupted by everything that White America instilled into him
So that he becomes a true soldier in the struggle for freedom and equality
And that's the de-programming of a niggatron.
Take control of your mind, brother
Use the knowledge
Never abuse it
Don't let anyone or anything change you

© 2009 Corey Ali Copeland

GLANCE INSIDE MY MIND

Glance inside this brother's mind and you will find…
A brother who is the true product of great Nubian kings and queens
Descended from the motherland
Africa
The great home of legendary warriors, tacticians and scholars
Where the origins of many academic subjects are from
The birthplace of nature with all its geographical splendors
Only to be subdued and replaced by Western culture with their corruptive and colonizing ways
Where our people are being taken away by European slave traders who only want to profit from our pain and suffering
Causing many great villages and provinces to be looted and plundered
So many people of their tribes will be lost without a place to be home
Glance inside this brother's mind and you will find…
A proud brother descended from great tribes who were taken as slaves captured on European ships on the horrible trial on the Middle Passage
Only to be stranded in a place which is not our own and being ripped of our own identity and heritage
Given slave names to be confuse and bamboozle us
Also, we were forced to learn all aspects of Western civilization
Asking themselves
"Where is our true self?"
It is being washed away by the waves of slavery and oppression
Lost like a pack of wolves searching for every stench of food
Still we were being put into cotton fields and whipped like dogs
Only to the make the plantation owners pleased by mistreating us
Like we are not important to them in the first place
Continuing to live under morbid conditions
Until we develop the strength and courage to break the shackles that have us bonded like malnourished rats in a cage
Then as we escaped from the killing fields
We have become soldiers
Scouts
Commanders
And political leaders
Great men and women of hope and dignity
Who will lead the way for us to build and endure in a land which its' people continue to despise us
Glance inside this brother's mind and you will find…
A modern day warrior in black leather
United with brothers with a coalition of the same purpose

Sisters roaming the streets with Nubian flair and Afros
Also with their clenched fists
Raising high....high....so high
Up up...in the sky
Panther power on the rampage
With a primal fury that is more powerful than a
Thundering blast from a 12 gauge shotgun
We are marching to the tribal beats and chants
Coming from the drums of our ancestors banging from the heavens above this wretched ball of confusion
Screaming the immortal words of revolution
Black Power! Black Power!
With raw emotion and pride
So that every corner of the world can hear and witness the coming of a new day
Glance inside this brother's mind and you will find....
A brother who has seen it all
All the nonsense that plague us in the past and again to continue oppressing us today
A young brother's life taken away in Howard Beach
Another being brutalized in L.A.
And another young Black soul lost in Bensonhurst
And then another one in Crown Heights
And another....
And then...
He can't take it to see
So much death and destruction
It makes a great people cry and moan in disbelief
Crying tears of sorrow into the earth
Until their souls will rise up to roam into the air
So now you see the torture and hatred that eight messed –up years of Bush-infested stupidity has gotten us
But thank God that we got a Black President who is getting things done
Now it is the time for a people to wake up and realize that we need to be even more vigilant than ever
Because even today in 2009
We are still targets of oppression and hate set upon by those who want to rid us from the fabric of global civilization
So glance into this brother's mind
This is of course, my mind
And please ask me what I find
The answer may surprise you.

© 2009 Corey Ali Copeland

I FEEL YOUR PAIN

To all of my sisters of the world who have been battered, bruised and stepped on
Scarred and maimed
Abused and misused
Also turned down by society and left for eternal insanity
Fed up and hopeless
I feel your pain
To all of my hard working professional sisters of the world who work, sweat and busted their asses for others who have a "God of Superiority" complex
While struggling to make a decent dollar for themselves and their families while….
Being trapped in a fuckin' jungle of food stamps and welfare
Like the system just don't seem to care
I feel your pain
To all of my talented sisters of the world whose gifts are being coerced and corrupted by these racist pimps in their 3-pieced business suits
Trying to change your originality into something that you mostly despised and then program your skills to enslaved into their web of greed and misery
Still yearning to remain free
For that, I feel your pain.
To all of my physically endowed sisters of the world who were forced from being totally pure souls into a state of idiotic exposure as people see you dancing, gyrating and degrading
Yet, you stoop so damn low to make a fast buck and gain your 15 minutes of fame
Ain't that a god damn shame?
But still, I feel your pain
To all of my strong minded sisters of the world who have been referred to not by as equals, queens, mothers, cousins, etc.
But instead many fools referred you as a hoe, skank, tramp and mostly a good for nothing Bitch!!
Don't these white devil controlled niggatrons know who you are?
But still you will never hear me utter those words to you
Seriously, I feel your pain
To every beautiful Black woman in the world who have been through so many obstacles of oppression and hate set upon by the Racist parasites who are so damn demented and deranged
Vying to halt the evolution of strength, beauty and grace who is YOU!
When you fall into their trap and there is no way out of its hell bent grasp
Be informed that you got real brothers who will stand by You!
Fight for you!
Willing to love you!
Cherish you!
Honor you!
Ready to make you
As the Queen in their lives
Because….we feel your pain

© 2009 Corey Ali Copeland

METAPHORS OF BLACKNESS

As the sun begins to come out of hiding from beyond the earth
We cam out of the fresh made soil as we start to slowly evolve like
The Most High Exalted created Adam and Eve
We instantly blossomed
Into the ripened fruit of our great civilization
As told in the legendary scrolls of our history
This legacy began in ancient Egyptian times
In the eras of Pharoahs and Queens
Where great names like
King Tut, Ramses, Nefertiti, Hapsuteut and Tutmose
Known ominous to most of our people
Who have built the Sphinx and the almighty Pyramids
Only to continue as an everlasting phase of a metamorphous
That travel through the scared corridors of time
Time…Time
In a time where we were taken from the land of great ancestry
Which is the Motherland!
In which we are stolen from its rich fields
Forced into the horrific Middle Passage to the New World
Only to be brutalized and downgraded by the
Plantation Big Cats…Slave Owners
The real devils filled with hate
Who made out lives a living hell for over 400 years
Still we slowly evolve as soldiers, warriors, tacticians and leaders
Also, and free men!
Free!
Free from the bondage which kept us barricaded and shackled
Like demonic savages from a horror movie
We were treated like god damn tourists from another country
And set aside from that punk ass Jim Crow and his good old boys
Uncle Sam and the dreaded Ku Klux Klan
Again, still we evolve as intellectual radicals and militants
Freedom fighters following the war cry of the Black Panthers
Reared by the philosophy of Brother Bobby
And the tactical rhetoric of sweet pretty Brother Huey
As we remained
Free at last as spoken by Brother Martin
And Brother Malcolm tell us to do
By Any Means Necessary
As we walk with the Red, Black and the Green
Waving it in White America's face

And screaming
Black Power! Black Power!
Loud and proud all over the place
With voices so loud that God and his angels could hear it
Yet we again evolve into self-righteous individuals
No!
Self righteous
Revolutionaries!
Who are iron-willed, dedicated and wise
To teach and guide the youth of today
Into the rights of passage
That our great ancestors and griots passed on into us
For that
We have witness a completion of
Struggle, Determination, Courage, Perseverance and Wisdom
Witness our brothers – educated, positive and wise
Witness our sisters – diligent, beautiful and regal
Take a glance at the final paradox
That we called
The Metaphors of Blackness
Black is Power
Black is Beautiful
The Blacker the berry
The sweeter the juice of the nectar
One Love
Sho'Nuff
Ya Dig!!!
Peace!!

© 2009 Corey Ali Copeland

I'M A BLACKMAN

You may see me in box braids or dread,
A clean natural cut or a nappy head.
You may see me in urban clothes or cultural wear,
An elegant tux or radical gear
I'm a black man as you can see.
A true black man – that is me.

You can look at my eyes they steely stare,
Dare to daze into them with confusion and despair.
You may notice me as a reject or a freak,
But I have a brain for thinking and a voice to speak
I'm a black man as you can see.
A true black man – that is me.

You may see as a plague or a disease,
But I have wisdom that put the wicked mind at ease.
You may notice me as nothing or a zero,
But don't you know I'm the same as you though.
I'm a black man as you can see
A true black man – that is me.

I can visualize the tragedy of my people's journey,
From the motherland to the new land,
their legacy flows through me.
I see through my eyes the pain and agony of my people's quest
For freedom and equality,
we will rise to the test.
Many blind fools today just can't see
That there is a black man just like me.

America, you shackled and whipped me to death,
Hung me on a noose to take my last breath.
My hatred and rage take aim at my oppressor,
who don't give a fuck about my cause nor care no lessor.
For of course, there is a black man as many can see
A black man who wants to be free.

So I don't want to hear about you being superior,
And dare to look at me as if I was inferior.
But for now, I'll stand in my militant stance.
To give Jim Crow one haymaker to the brain,

If given a chance.

For they know not to hold back a Black man, for they can see
A proud black man – that is me

© 1994 Corey Ali Copeland

SISTER LONA

This poem is dedicated to the memory of Lona M. Williams, Boys And Girls High School Class of '88

Sister Lona
You are one of those dear folks
Who is mostly well liked
Very well mannered
And highly intelligent
With the face of a model
The mind of a genius
And the heart of a saint
You have touched so many lives with your smile, grace and caring personality
You are truly blessed with the ability to assist those who do not have a friend
Becoming a mentor to those who do not have no one to look up to
And becoming a popular soul whose memories will be etched in the halls of the High.
Ever since you came to this legendary institution
You have encouraged many people with your undying compassion and wisdom
Even many dumb-founded students come to you because you are one heck of a math tutor
Your patient and sweet demeanor of helping others has made you the heroine of the mathematically illiterate
I mean you show them to face their fears in dealing with variables, expressions, integers, multiples, dividends, etc.
The whole algebraic spectrum in general!
Even you look like a college professor
You have the dreams, the desire
and the determination to be whatever you can be
You are a very special kind of individual
A true friend and a special person who is a true blessing in disguise
You are one of the true legends of the Dream Class
But now that you're gone
And God had summoned you to be become one of his precious angels
Always remember one thing
That you will be forever loved by your family and friends
Right here on Earth
May you eternally watch us always up there in Heaven
Until then
See you at the crossroads, my friend.

See you at the crossroads.

© 2009 Corey Ali Copeland

STREAMS: Ancestral Point of Consciousness Rising

Looking back, looking forward
Looking back at our past, our legacy
During our history, we were treated like savages, outcasts and nomads
Raped of our culture, creativity and mostly our freedom
We have been whipped and tortured like wild dogs without a leash
Shackled down from our wrists to our swollen ankles by those who want control our destiny, our heritage, our way of life and force us into being
Humiliated, manipulated, hated by, spitted, beat on and being exploited
Like those actors and actresses we seen on TV and in the movies
The powers that be leaving us Powerless without a sense of who we are, what we are and where are we going to now!
But as the spirits of the ancestors look upon this wretched planet and they say "it's time for our people to be Free!"
Free from the pain and suffering of slavery that has bestowed us for over 400 years as We Look Forward!
Free from the hell-bent damnation of the slave master who profit greatly from our blood, sweat and tears as We Look Forward!
Free from being everyday targets or will become victims of Jim Crowism and the racist Klansman's grasp as We Look Forward!
Free to be human beings with the same rights and equality instead of being savages trapped in rat and roach infested cages as We Look Forward!
And mostly, free so we thank the ancestral spirits that watch us sharply and guide us with their strength, dedication, determination, love and wisdom as We Look Forward!
From this day, we have become more powerful, more determined, more focused and wiser than ever.
As warriors in this millennium, we must keep fighting until all ghosts of fears and hate flee from our souls so that we continue to look and move forward!
Move on, my brother! Move on, my sister! Move on, my people!
Look ahead to the future, my comrades!
Move on, move on, Move On!!!!

© 2007 Corey Ali Copeland

WE ARE THE DREAM CLASS

This poem is dedicated to the Boys and Girls High School Class of 1988

We were students
We were teachers
We were classmates
Teammates,
Family,
Friends,
Comrades,
But most of all,
We were mature individuals
We strive for nothing but excellence,
We carefully plan for our futures
We all willing to go all the way
To better ourselves academically,
Socially,
And Spiritually.
We never think about using any other alternative to succeed
We accept many challenges
Physically,
Intellectually,
Mentally,
And morally.
We excel on achieving our goals
And willing to assist those
Who want to become great
To do better and to be the best
We persevere in attaining our objectives
We listen carefully to our teachers
Gain advice from our counselors
And more importantly,
We honor and respect our principal
Yet,
We are different kinds of people
We have our moments
Whether it's good,
Bad,
Funny,
Or sometimes hysterical.
We even have our wildest experiences
And our most tender moments.
But even though we are still
Young, eager, vibrant and full of energy
We have become responsible young adults

With vision, compassion and courage
We accept the academic mission set upon by our teachers
We stand and heed the call
And we set the standards
For others to follow
Still we work hard and study harder
We have fun
Share laughs
And grasp for the good life
But we never stray away from
Our ultimate goal..........Success
With that heart
With that drive
With that determination and desire
We went to become
Lawyers,
Nurses,
Teachers,
Engineers,
Administrators,
Accountants,
Programmers,
Entrepreneurs,
And even Artists.
And now over 20 years later,
As we gather together once again,
We have come to remember
The faces we know
The friends we have and the times that we share
For we set the mark for future graduating classes to follow.
We are the hope and not the fear
We are the leaders and not the followers
We are the originators and not the imitators
We are the shining crown jewel of the High
We are the products of a true urban institute of learning that stands proudly in Central Brooklyn
We are the educational cream of the crop
We are the true Pride and Joy of Bedford Stuyvesant
We are the Boys and Girls High School Class of nineteen hundred eighty-eight
We are the Dream Class
We are the Dream Class
We are
The Dream Class!
Eighty-Eight for Life!

© 2009 Corey Ali Copeland

WHEN BLACK PEOPLE RULE THE WORLD

When Black people rule the world (shout three times)

When black people rule the world
Brothers and sisters will come together as one bounded united front
Stronger than the combination of steel and any form of metal
Link as they form an unbreakable chain of unity
Never to be broken or separated by any kind of hatred and confusion
Build by the undying commitment and love that they will pass onto
The youth
So they can become a much stronger force
To reach, teach and liberate
Those who can not liberate and uplift themselves

When Black people rule the world (shout three times)

When black people rule the world
Crackheads, winos and bums will witness the coming of
The clean shaven educated brother
As they begin to develop a new conscience of self-awareness
Picking up books and speeches from Muhammad, Malcolm, Martin,
Marcus, Langston, Countee, Richard, Claude and other literary giants
No!
Legends who wrote more than just words
But scared blueprints designed to not only change the man
But to mold him mentally, psychologically, spiritually and morally
Instead of continuing to be mindless Niggatrons programmed to hate and kill
For the new wave slave master
They can be full bloodied
Revolutionaries
With a strong sense of Black pride and not being afraid of being
Bold
And Beautiful

When Black people rule the world (shout three times)

When black people rule the world
Our children will be taught real African history by
Fully educated real radical scholars
Instead of being misled by
These misguided dumb ass Harvard trained educators who wanted to
Educate
Or perpetrate
Our youth's minds with some bullshit
That doesn't have

Anything
To do with us
All these hypocrites still getting us to believe that
Columbus, Polo, Galileo and all these motherfuckers
Claim that they made world history
But still these damn fools forgot to mention
Songahy Ali, Askia The Great, Chaka Zulu, Nefertiti, King Tut…
Great African leaders who made true world history
Real heroes and sheroes who are warriors, strategists, architects, scribes and so on.
And these should be a law to find and shoot any racist scum and Bush loving
Sellout and
Dare call us Nigger in front of us!
Knowing that We Are Not Niggers!
We are native sons and daughters of a great civilization
Gifted with the will to survive

When Black people rule the world (shout three times)

When black people rule the world
The colors of the American flag, a symbol of a country
Which enslaved us like the fuckin' animals in a filthy zoo?
Rape and torture us for over the last 400 years
And is still continuing
Robbed us of our blood, our sweat and our tears
Treated my mother and sisters like they are not second class bitches
Which they are not!
Uncle Sam and his good ol' boys will be scared as shit coming out of their stinkin' asses
Funking up the whole country with their Klan-liked influence and demented thought
process
But we are so glad that there is a brother in the White House
Who is getting things done despite what right-wing and conservatives think
And we, as true warriors – we're gonna straighten things out
By changing the fucked up U.S. Constitution into a Black list of Laws which will cater to
only us
And also make the Capitol into a citadel of Black Power
That is Black unity times two
So what the hell you cross-burning, White cloth wearing, nigger-lynching Dixie bastards
gonna do?
Nothing!
Better pray for your eternal downfall

When Black people rule the world (shout three times)

When black people rule the world
The ghettos which we roamed all of our lives will be national landmarks
Every liquor store, number spot and crack house will throw out their entire inventory

And replace them with books and materials
To give to a new breed of revolutionary
The powerful colors of the African National Flag
The Red, the Black and the Green
Will rise higher than God himself
Flying over every city in a wasteland called America
And there should be a national holiday to celebrate the birthday of Reverend Al Sharpton
Kwanzaa should be a legal week long cultural celebration
Still we can have to the strength to refrain our mindset from this bullshit called
The American Dream
Which is still an ever-ongoing nightmare for us

When Black people rule the world (shout three times)

O'Reilly and Scarborough will get pimp slapped by the Black fist on national T.V.
Fat ass Rush Limbaugh will get beat up by Mo'Nique in a cat fight
Brothers and sisters who were incarcerated will cause a global ruckus and spark a brand new revolution
When their clenched fists and high voices rise up in the midnight air
Telling the world to Wake the Fuck up!!!

When Black people rule the world (shout three times)

But until then....
We are still partying (and dying)
Bullshiting (and dying)
Crying (and dying)
Losing our minds (and dying)
Losing our souls (and dying)
Dying, dying, dying and dying....

Question is...Are you ready for change if Black people rule the world?

© 2007 Corey Ali Copeland

STUMBLING

During these rough and turbulent times
No matter how hard it is to survive
Or what obstacles stand in your path to righteousness
You got to walk on a straight line in this hell hole called reality
Trying you hardest not to stumble
Stumbling
Like a wino drowning in his death bed of booze and despair
Walking without purpose on a dead end street
Seeking his last sip of Thunderbird to hide his senseless rant to every decent hard working brother walking on his block
Stumbling
Like a hopeless basehead with his eyes stoned out
Looking like an infected zombie from a horror movie
Seeking for an ounce of meth or any other drug to support his habit of terrifying
Every unexpected soul for their money
Brother
You got to continue focusing and not stumble out of place
Stumbling
Like a young prostitute fine as hell
Strutting on the corner in the wee hours
Spreading her sexy legs for her juicy pussy to entice every hard dick to fuck her until she gets a brother's dough
While she is struggling to put food on the table for her children
Trying to get them out of the ghetto
Stumbling
Like a lost soul misguided by religious confusion
Trying to find the right way back to the Lord to be saved again
Like a brother in a dark alley
Trying so damn hard to remain focused and determined
Without being swayed to bullshit, foolishness and strife
While walking straight on a thin line without the knack to stumble
Stumbling
Like a young wannabe thug sticking up everyone in the hood
Until he slowly realize that his 15 minutes of fame will only put him
In a motherfuckin' hall of shame
Stuck inside a prison cell
Surrounded by four side of iron bars
Yet, we still try to walk straight but we still
Stumbling
Like a bunch of dominoes tumbling down on a table
Just like two former super powers used to declare who is mightier

Who is the mighty on with the mouth
The money,
The machines of war
Or even
Who is the one with the iron fist?
All those questions still stumbling
Stumbling
Stumbling….Stumbling
Stumbling in my mind
Until I trip and fall and hurt myself with ignorance and doubt
Try to pick myself again and walk even steadier and stronger
And God Allah only come to guide me
Into the righteous path
So please
Lord of lords
King of kings
Grant me the will and the wisdom to become the hope of hopes
The soul of souls and the poetic voice of voices to those without a cause
Without desire
Without determination
Without substance
And
Without a creative talent of putting emotions on paper
So my people can become free of the god damn slave concept which plagues them for so long
Teach them to be
A people with a legacy
With a purpose
With a sense of justice
With a sense of pride
Moreover,
Teach them to always walk steady and strong
Instead being thoughtless living corpses who have nothing on their empty mind but to continue stumbling without living
Stumbling without living
Stumbling….Stumbling
Stumbling

© 2009 Corey Ali Copeland

WHAT IS REVOLUTION?

A lot of brothers and sisters are lost and confused in this new decade
They don't realize that without change
They would not have better chances in obtaining a job
Obtaining an education
Or even living the American Dream

But in order to get the change that we as a people
Who had been suffering and struggling for over 400 years
We need more than a handout
A ten year plan
Or even assistance from the Government
We need a........

REVOLUTION!

So what is revolution?

To me....

Revolution is brothers and sisters coming together
Collaborating their thoughts to make a change
And make a stand against any form of racist oppression

Revolution is brothers and sisters speaking with their voices
Loud and proud
To spread their powerful messages of liberation to a massive crowd.

What is revolution?

Revolution is our children and our young people
Demanding what they want to learn
Parents and guardians of our children getting strongly involved with
Local and national issues and problems that show them much concern.

Revolution is our brothers and sisters in the higher institutions of learning
As in colleges and universities
Armed with the intangible wit and honed skills to gain power to get
what they want and need to strive for to become in the final hour

What is revolution?

Revolution is brothers and sisters wearing Black shirts and jackets
Leathered and button down
Matched with Black boots zipped up
Ready to go back to their roots

And what is REVOLUTION?!!!!

Revolution is payback for over the last four hundred years
Robbing us
Of our blood,
Our sweat,
And our tears

Now you understand that.....

Revolution is our time
Because we elected a Black man in the White House
Revolution is our destiny
Because we waited generations and generations to shine in the spotlight
Revolution is our scared place in history
Because we will teach and pass on our legacy to the next generation

And that is what Revolution is......

That's Revolution to me.

© 2010 Corey Ali Copeland

About The Author

Born and raised in the Bedford Stuyvesant section of Brooklyn, New York, Brother Ali-Hotep (a.k.a. Corey Ali Copeland) has began his poetic journey in 1991 with the same Black Revolutionary rhetoric echoed in the legendary works of Gil Scott-Heron, Nikki Giovanni, Amiri Baraka, Maya Angelou and The Last Poets. His works including the meaning of Black consciousness, self-awareness and social uprising. In the following months, he is planning to work on several books, which contains more of his outstanding poetic genius.

Brother Ali-Hotep now resides in the Bushwick section of Brooklyn, but still considers Bed-Stuy home. He is an alumni of Boys and Girls High School and an alumni of New York City College of Technology of the City University of New York with an AAS in Advertising Design and an Bachelor's degree in Communication Design.

Brother Ali-Hotep has performed at several poetry venues in New York City including the Afrikan Poetry Theatre in Jamaica, Queens; The Soul Sweet Sanctuary in the Bronx and Food 4 Thought Juice Bar & Cafe in Brooklyn.

Manufactured by Amazon.ca
Acheson, AB